1 2 JUL 2021

Early Readers

'The Gnome Who Roamed'

An original concept by Heather Pindar

© Heather Pindar

Illustrated by Juliana Cuervo

Published by MAVERICK ARTS PUBLISHING LTD

Studio 11, City Business Centre, 6 Brighton Road,

Horsham, West Sussex, RH13 5BB

© Maverick Arts Publishing Limited November 2020

+44 (0)1403 256941

A CIP catalogue record for this book is available at the British Library.

ISBN 978-1-84886-724-6

www.maverickbooks.co.uk

This book is rated as: White Band (Guided Reading)

The Gnome Who Roamed

By Heather Pindar

Illustrated by
Juliana Cuervo

Chapter 1

Jerome Gnome loved to roam. He had wanted to be an explorer since he was knee-high to a mushroom, which is very small indeed.

So far he had only roamed on the banks of the river next to his house. But he wanted to roam much, much further.

One sunny morning, he packed his torch, map and compass in his bag.

"I'm going roaming!" he called to his mum.

"Have fun! Happy roaming, Jerome," she called back without looking up from her book. His brothers and sisters waved and carried on with their fishing game.

Jerome walked across a field. He climbed through a small gap in a hedge. He was next to a busy road. A woman in a smart purple jumper

was standing next to a sign with a picture of a bus on it. There was a large paper bag at her feet.

What Jerome saw next made him very excited indeed.

Just peeping above the top of the bag, Jerome could see... another gnome!

'Another Roaming Gnome like me!' thought Jerome. 'How clever he is! He's climbed inside that bag so he can roam a very long way.'

A large yellow bus arrived. Jerome took a deep breath. He crept into the bag with the other roaming gnome.

Jerome's tummy did a somersault as he felt the paper bag being lifted onto the bus.

The woman put the bag down. Jerome looked at the other gnome. He was very still. He was holding a fishing rod tightly. He didn't even look at Jerome.

"Hello, I'm Jerome," he whispered. "Please may I roam with you?"

The other gnome didn't answer.

'That's a bit rude,' thought Jerome, but he didn't give up easily.

"Do you roam often?" asked Jerome. Still the other gnome stared ahead. Jerome gently tapped the gnome's shoulder. It felt hard and cold. Very strange.

Now Jerome understood the truth; this gnome was a stone gnome, not a Real Live Roaming Gnome like Jerome.

Chapter 2

After a lot of bumping, the bus stopped. Jerome felt the bag zoom upwards again as the woman carried it off the bus and into a big building.

"I want to change this boring Fishing Gnome for a Barbecuing Gnome please," she said. She pulled out the stone gnome.

Jerome peeped over the top of the bag. "Oh!" she said. "That's strange. There's an extra gnome in my bag."

"He must have fallen in there," said the shop assistant. "I'll pop him back outside."

Jerome felt two firm hands grab him around his middle and carry him off. He just managed to stop himself from wriggling and calling out.

The shop assistant carried Jerome outside and put him down on a low shelf. All around him were rows of still, silent gnomes. Some people were walking on the path in front of him.

Jerome tried to remember his *Gnoming Code* – the list of rules that help gnomes in their everyday lives. He remembered Gnoming Rule Number 1: *Freeze if you see a human.*

Jerome looked straight ahead. He stood as still as the stone gnomes. He stayed still when a pigeon flew up and sat down on his hat. He stood still until the people went away, and everything went dark.

Jerome shivered. He took out his torch. Now he could go exploring and find a way out.

Jerome walked along the path. He saw lots of plants. He saw big pots, sheds and ponds. At the end of the path there was a high green fence. Jerome looked left and right. It seemed to go on forever.

Jerome sighed and began to walk slowly back along the path. Suddenly he remembered Gnoming Rule Number 2: *If it's all going wrong, sing a song.*

Jerome began to sing his favourite song...
"*Gnome free! Free as the mushrooms grow...*"

Then Jerome heard another voice.

"*Roam free! Free as the rivers flow...*"

Someone was joining in with his song!

"Hello, is there a Real Live Gnome out there?"

"Yes. My name's Colin," said a cheery voice.
"Pleased to meet you."

Jerome shone his torch
towards the voice. "I'm
Jerome," he said, "And I'm
very, *very* pleased to meet
you!" Jerome sat down
next to Colin.

"I was looking for the way out," he said.

"Oh dear," said Colin. "The only way to get out of the garden centre is to be bought by someone."

"So this is a garden centre! I've heard of them in stories. Do you like it here, Colin?"

"It's alright. But I'd rather live in a proper garden with a shed. I've been hoping someone would buy me, but they never do."

"Hmm," said Jerome thoughtfully. "I see you're a Fishing Gnome. I don't wish to be rude, but there are a lot of Fishing Gnomes. I've heard some people find them a little bit... um... boring."

"Yes. I'd like to be one of those Barbecuing Gnomes," said Colin. "They're really popular."

Jerome rubbed his hands together. "Maybe you *can* be one."

Chapter 3

The next day, Jerome stood close to Colin on the low shelf. Colin was wearing a chef's hat and carrying a long fork. Jerome was still holding his compass, torch and map to show he was a serious Roaming Gnome.

People started walking along the path again. The annoying pigeon came back and pecked his feet.

"Get off!" he hissed, but the pigeon took no notice.

Around lunchtime, a small girl with short dark hair came to look at the gnomes. Jerome remembered Rule Number 3 of the Gnoming Code: *Humans under 10 can usually be trusted.*

Jerome looked up at the girl. He took off his hat and bowed. "Hello. I'm Jerome. I'm a Real Live Roaming Gnome. Pleased to meet you."

The little girl stared. "You're a real live gnome?"

"Yes, I am. I'm also in a little bit of trouble. This is my friend, Colin. We're stuck here. We need someone to buy us, so we can escape."

"Oh. I haven't got any money," said the girl.

A tall man with a grey beard walked over and stood next to the girl.

"I didn't know you liked gnomes, Charlotte," he said. "Would you like one to take home?"

"Oh yes please, Grandpa! I want these two gnomes," said Charlotte, pointing at Colin and Jerome.

"One gnome is plenty," said Grandpa. "Choose one."

Charlotte bit her lip. "I'll have this Roaming Gnome," she said. "Thank you, Grandpa!"

Grandpa reached down to pick up Jerome. Suddenly Jerome remembered Gnoming Rule Number 4: *A gnome in need is a friend indeed.* Jerome must help Colin! He linked arms with Colin and held on tight.

"Oh," said Grandpa as he lifted Jerome and Colin. "These two are stuck together. They must come as a pair."

Chapter 4

Charlotte put Jerome and Collin down in a corner of her garden. It was full of flowers. The grass was long. Dragonflies flew over the pond and around the brightly painted shed. Charlotte came to talk with Jerome and Colin as often as she could.

"This is great!" said Colin a few days after they arrived. "I love the pond. I love Charlotte. And the shed! Especially the shed. I don't ever want to leave here."

"It is great," said Jerome. "But I want to go home. I've checked my map. Look! There's a river not far from Charlotte's house. If I float down the river, it will take me all the way back to my house."

Jerome talked to Charlotte about his plan. She came back later with some shiny pink arm bands.

"They're to help you float," she said.

Jerome put on the arm bands and his backpack. He shook hands with Colin. He threw his arms around Charlotte's knees. "Goodbye," he said, "I'll visit you soon."

Charlotte and Colin waved sadly as Jerome set off.

Chapter 5

The river was wide and cold. Jerome bobbed along quickly in the water. He felt something land on his head. The pigeon from the garden centre was pooing on his hat.

Jerome remembered Gnoming Rule Number 5: *Your hat has more uses than you know.* He felt glad that he hardly ever took it off.

Just as Jerome's arms were beginning to get tired, Jerome saw his house beside the river. He tried to swim towards it, but the river was too fast. He remembered Gnoming Rule Number 5 again. He took off his hat and waved it.

"Hello, hello!" he shouted. His whole family ran out of the house and into the river. They grabbed Jerome's arms and helped him climb out.

"Thanks!" said Jerome. "Were you all worried about me?"

"No, not really," said his mum. "Remember Gnoming Rule Number 24: *Pigeons are smarter than they look.*"

"Rule 24!" said Jerome. "There's lots *more* Gnoming Rules?"

"Oh yes," said his mum, "104 Gnoming Rules I think, at the last count. Our Gnoming Pigeon told us you were okay. And anyway, why worry?

We heard you're a proper Real Live Roaming Gnome now."

"I love to roam," said Jerome. "But I'll always come home."

"I'm glad," said his mum. "Hmm, have you thought about washing that hat?"

The End

Book Bands for Guided Reading

The Institute of Education book banding system is a scale of colours that reflects the various levels of reading difficulty. The bands are assigned by taking into account the content, the language style, the layout and phonics. Word, phrase and sentence level work is also taken into consideration.

Maverick Early Readers are a bright, attractive range of books covering the pink to white bands. All of these books have been book banded for guided reading to the industry standard and edited by a leading educational consultant.

To view the whole Maverick Readers scheme, visit our website at

www.maverickearlyreaders.com

Or scan the QR code above to view our scheme instantly!

Pink
Red
Yellow
Blue
Green
Orange
Turquoise
Purple
Gold
White